SELECTED POEMS

SELECTED POEMS

BY

WALTER DE LA MARE

NEW YORK
HENRY HOLT AND COMPANY

To

CHARLES AND VIRGINIA HOWLAND

The poems in this volume have been chosen from *The Listeners*, *Poems* (1904), *Flora*, *Motley*, *The Veil*, and *Crossing* (a play).

Nothing has been included from the volumes intended for children; namely, *Songs of Childhood*, *Peacock Pie*, *A Child's Day*, *Down-Adown-Derry*; or from *Ding Dong Bell*.

CONTENTS

Contents

Contents

SELECTED POEMS

TITMOUSE

If you would happy company win,
Dangle a palm-nut from a tree,
Idly in green to sway and spin,
Its snow-pulped kernel for bait; and see,
 A nimble titmouse enter in.

Out of earth's vast unknown of air,
Out of all summer, from wave to wave,
He'll perch, and prank his feathers fair,
Jangle a glass-clear wildering stave,
 And take his commons there —

This tiny son of life; this spright,
By momentary Human sought,
Plume will his wing in the dappling light,
Clash timbrel shrill and gay —
And into Time's enormous nought,
 Sweet-fed, will flit away.

· 3 ·

THE LINNET

Upon this leafy bush
   With thorns and roses in it,
Flutters a thing of light,
   A twittering linnet;
And all the throbbing world
   Of dew and sun and air
By this small parcel of life
   Is made more fair;
As if each bramble-spray
And mounded gold-wreathed furze,
   Harebell and little thyme,
   Were only hers;
As if this beauty and grace
   Did to one bird belong,
And, at a flutter of wing,
   Might vanish in song.

THE WILLOW

Leans now the fair willow, dreaming
Amid her locks of green.
In the driving snow she was parched and cold,
And in midnight hath been
Swept by blasts of void night,
Lashed by the rains.
Now of that wintry dark and bleak
No memory remains.

In mute desire she sways softly;
Thrilling sap up-flows;
She praises God in her beauty and grace;
Whispers delight; and there flows
A delicate wind from the Southern seas,
Kissing her leaves.   She sighs.
While the birds in her tresses make merry;
Burns the Sun in the skies.

THREE CHERRY TREES

There were three cherry trees once,
  Grew in a garden all shady;
And there for delight of so gladsome a sight,
  Walked a most beautiful lady,
  Dreamed a most beautiful lady.

Birds in those branches did sing,
  Blackbird and throstle and linnet,
But she walking there was by far the most fair —
  Lovelier than all else within it,
  Blackbird and throstle and linnet.

But blossoms to berries do come,
  All hanging on stalks light and slender,
And one long summer's day charmed that lady
        away,
  With vows sweet and merry and tender;
  A lover with voice low and tender.

· 6 ·

Moss and lichen the green branches deck;
Weeds nod in its paths green and shady:
Yet a light footstep seems there to wander in
    dreams,
  The ghost of that beautiful lady,
  That happy and beautiful lady.

NOON AND NIGHT FLOWER

Not any flower that blows
But shining watch doth keep;
Every swift changing chequered hour it knows
Now to break forth in beauty; now to sleep.

This for the roving bee
Keeps open house, and this
Stainless and clear is, that in darkness she
May lure the moth to where her nectar is.

Lovely beyond the rest
Are these of all delight: —
The tiny pimpernel that noon loves best,
The primrose palely burning through the night.

One 'neath day's ardent sky
With ruby decks her place,
The other when Eve's chariot glides by
Lifts her dim torch to light that dreaming face.

· 8 ·

THE BELLS

Shadow and light both strove to be
The eight bell-ringers' company,
As with his gliding rope in hand,
Counting his changes, each did stand;
While rang and trembled every stone,
To music by the bell-mouths blown:
Till the bright clouds that towered on high
Seemed to re-echo cry with cry.
Still swang the clappers to and fro,
When, in the far-spread fields below,
I saw a ploughman with his team
Lift to the bells and fix on them
His distant eyes, as if he would
Drink in the utmost sound he could;
While near him sat his children three,
And in the green grass placidly
Played undistracted on, as if
What music earthly bells might give
Could only faintly stir their dream,

And stillness make more lovely seem.
Soon night hid horses, children, all
In sleep deep and ambrosial.
Yet, yet, it seemed, from star to star,
Welling now near, now faint and far,
Those echoing bells rang on in dream,
And stillness made even lovelier seem.

THE SCARECROW

All winter through I bow my head
    Beneath the driving rain;
The North Wind powders me with snow
    And blows me back again;
At midnight 'neath a maze of stars
    I flame with glittering rime,
And stand, above the stubble, stiff
    As mail at morning-prime.
But when that child, called Spring, and all
    His host of children, come,
Scattering their buds and dew upon
    These acres of my home,
Some rapture in my rags awakes;
    I lift void eyes and scan
The skies for crows, those ravening foes,
    Of my strange master, Man.
I watch him striding lank behind
    His clashing team, and know

Soon will the wheat swish body high
   Where once lay sterile snow;
Soon shall I gaze across a sea
   Of sun-begotten grain,
Which my unflinching watch hath sealed
   For harvest once again.

NOD

Softly along the road of evening,
  In a twilight dim with rose,
Wrinkled with age, and drenched with dew,
  Old Nod, the shepherd, goes.

His drowsy flock streams on before him,
  Their fleeces charged with gold,
To where the sun's last beam leans low
  On Nod the shepherd's fold.

The hedge is quick and green with brier,
  From their sand the conies creep;
And all the birds that fly in heaven
  Flock singing home to sleep.

His lambs outnumber a noon's roses,
  Yet, when night's shadows fall,
His blind old sheep-dog, Slumber-soon,
  Misses not one of all.

His are the quiet steeps of dreamland,
    The waters of no-more-pain,
His ram's bell rings 'neath an arch of stars,
    "Rest, rest, and rest again."

ENGLAND

No lovelier hills than thine have laid
  My tired thoughts to rest;
No peace of lovelier valleys made
  Like peace within my breast.

Thine are the woods whereto my soul,
  Out of the noontide beam,
Flees for a refuge green and cool
  And tranquil as a dream.

Thy breaking seas like trumpets peal;
  Thy clouds — how oft have I
Watched their bright towers of silence steal
  Into infinity!

My heart within me faints to roam
  In thought even far from thee:
Thine be the grave whereto I come,
  And thine my darkness be.

HAUNTED

The rabbit in his burrow keeps
No guarded watch, in peace he sleeps;
The wolf that howls in challenging night
Cowers to her lair at morning light;
The simplest bird entwines a nest
Where she may lean her lovely breast,
Couched in the silence of the bough.
But thou, O man, what rest hast thou?

Thy emptiest solitude can bring
Only a subtler questioning
In thy divided heart. Thy bed
Recalls at dawn what midnight said.
Seek how thou wilt to feign content,
Thy flaming ardour's quickly spent;
Soon thy last company is gone,
And leaves thee — with thyself — alone.

Pomp and great friends may hem thee round,
A thousand busy tasks be found;
Earth's thronging beauties may beguile
Thy longing lovesick heart awhile;
And pride, like clouds of sunset, spread
A changing glory round thy head;
But fade will all; and thou must come,
Hating thy journey, homeless, home.

Rave how thou wilt; unmoved, remote,
That inward presence slumbers not,
Frets out each secret from thy breast,
Gives thee no rally, pause, nor rest,
Scans close thy very thoughts, lest they
Should sap his patient power away,
Answers thy wrath with peace, thy cry
With tenderest taciturnity.

A RIDDLE

The mild noon air of Spring again
Lapped shimmering in that sea-lulled lane.
Hazel was budding; wan as snow
The leafless blackthorn was a-blow.

A chaffinch clankt, a robin woke
An eerie stave in the leafless oak.
Green mocked at green; lichen and moss
The rain-worn slate did softly emboss.

From out her winter lair, at sigh
Of the warm South wind, a butterfly
Stepped, quaffed her honey; on painted fan
Her labyrinthine flight began.

Wondrously solemn, golden and fair,
The high sun's rays beat everywhere;
Yea, touched my cheek and mouth, as if,
Equal with stone, to me 'twould give
Its light and life.

O restless thought
Contented not.   With 'Why' distraught.
Whom asked you then your riddle small? —
'If hither came no man at all

Through this grey-green, sea-haunted lane,
Would it mere blackened nought remain?
Strives it this beauty and life to express
Only in human consciousness?'

Oh, rather, idly breaks he in
To an Eden innocent of sin;
And, prouder than to be afraid,
Forgets his Maker in the made.

BEFORE DAWN

Dim-berried is the mistletoe
With globes of sheenless grey;
The holly mid ten thousand thorns
Smoulders its fires away;
And in the manger Jesu sleeps
    This Christmas day.

Bull unto bull with hollow throat
Makes echo every hill,
Cold sheep in pastures thick with snow
The air with bleatings fill;
While of His mother's heart this Babe
    Takes His sweet will.

All flowers and butterflies lie hid,
The blackbird and the thrush
Pipe but a little as they flit
Restless from bush to bush;
Even to the robin Gabriel hath
    Cried softly, "Hush!"

Now night is astir with burning stars
In darkness of the snow;
Burdened with frankincense and myrrh
And gold the Strangers go
Into a dusk where one dim lamp
    Burns faintly, Lo!

No snowdrop yet its small head nods,
In winds of winter drear;
No lark at casement in the sky
Sings matins shrill and clear;
Yet in this frozen mirk the Dawn
    Breathes, Spring is here!

INNOCENCY

Like an old battle, youth is wild
With bugle and spear, and counter cry,
Fanfare and drummery, yet a child
Dreaming of that sweet chivalry,
The piercing terror cannot see.

He, with a mild and serious eye
Along the azure of the years,
Sees the sweet pomp sweep hurtling by;
But he sees not death's blood and tears,
Sees not the plunging of the spears.

And all the strident horror of
Horse and rider, in red defeat,
Is only music fine enough
To lull him into slumber sweet
In fields where ewe and lambkin bleat.

O, if with such simplicity
Himself take arms and suffer war;
With beams his targe shall gilded be,
Though in the thickening gloom be far
The steadfast light of any star!

Though hoarse War's eagle on him perch,
Quickened with guilty lightnings — there
It shall in vain for terror search,
Where a child's eyes 'neath bloody hair
Gaze purely through the dingy air.

And when the wheeling rout is spent,
Though in the heaps of slain he lie;
Or lonely in his last content;
Quenchless shall burn in secrecy
The flame Death knows his victors by.

THE MIRACLE

Who beckons the green ivy up
Its solitary tower of stone?
What spirit lures the bindweed's cup
      Unfaltering on?
Calls even the starry lichen to climb
By agelong inches endless Time?

Who bids the holyhock uplift
Her rod of fast-sealed buds on high;
Fling wide her petals — silent, swift,
      Lovely to the sky?
Since as she kindled, so she will fade,
Flower above flower in squalor laid.

Ever the heavy billow rears
All its sea-length in green, hushed wall;
But totters as the shore it nears,
      Foams to its fall;
Where was its mark? on what vain quest
Rose that great water from its rest?

So creeps ambition on; so climb
Man's vaunting thoughts.   He, set on high,
Forgets his birth, small space, brief time,
      That he shall die;
Dreams blindly in his dark, still air;
Consumes his strength; strips himself bare;

Rejects delight, ease, pleasure, hope,
Seeking in vain, but seeking yet,
Past earthly promise, earthly scope,
      On one aim set:
As if, like Chaucer's child, he thought
      All but "O Alma!" nought.

SOTTO VOCE
(TO EDWARD THOMAS)

The haze of noon wanned silver-grey,
The soundless mansion of the sun;
The air made visible in his ray,
Like molten glass from furnace run,
Quivered o'er heat-baked turf and stone
And the flower of the gorse burned on —
Burned softly as gold of a child's fair hair
Along each spiky spray, and shed
Almond-like incense in the air
Whereon our senses fed.

At foot — a few sparse harebells: blue
And still as were the friend's dark eyes
That dwelt on mine, transfixèd through
With sudden ecstatic surmise.

"Hst!" he cried softly, smiling, and lo,
Stealing amidst that maze gold-green —
I heard a whispering music flow
From a guileful throat of bird, unseen —
So delicate the straining ear
Scarce carried its faint syllabling

Into a heart caught-up to hear
That inmost pondering
Of bird-like self with self. We stood,
In happy trance-like solitude,
Hearkening a lullay grieved and sweet —
As when on isle uncharted beat
'Gainst coral at the palm-tree's root,
With brine-clear, snow-white foam afloat,
The wailing, not of water or wind —
A husht, far, wild, divine lament,
When Prospero his wizardry bent
Winged Ariel to bind . . .

Then silence, and o'er-flooding noon.
I raised my head; smiled too. And he —
Moved his great hand, the magic gone —
Gently amused to see
My ignorant wonderment. He sighed.
"It was a nightingale," he said,
"That *sotto voce* cons the song
He'll sing when dark is spread;
And Night's vague hours are sweet and long,
And we are laid abed."

MISTRESS FELL

"Whom seek you here, sweet Mistress Fell?"
"One who loved me passing well.
Dark his eye, wild his face —
Stranger, if in this lonely place
Bide such an one, then, prythee, say
I am come here to-day."

"Many his like, Mistress Fell?"
"I did not look, so cannot tell.
Only this I surely know,
When his voice called me, I must go;
Touched me his fingers, and my heart
Leapt at the sweet pain's smart."

"Why did he leave you, Mistress Fell?"
"Magic laid its dreary spell. —
Stranger, he was fast asleep;
Into his dream I tried to creep;
Called his name, soft was my cry;
He answered — not one sigh.

"The flower and the thorn are here;
Falleth they night-dew, cold and clear;
Out of her bower the bird replies,
Mocking the dark with ecstasies,
See how the earth's green grass doth grow,
Praising what sleeps below!

"Thus have they told me.   And I come,
As flies the wounded wild-bird home.
Not tears I give; but all that he
Clasped in his arms' sweet charity;
All that he loved — to him I bring
For a close whispering."

SLEEP

Men all, and birds, and creeping beasts,
  When the dark of night is deep,
From the moving wonder of their lives
  Commit themselves to sleep.

Without a thought, or fear, they shut
  The narrow gates of sense;
Heedless and quiet, in slumber turn
  Their strength to impotence.

The transient strangeness of the earth
  Their spirits no more see:
Within a silent gloom withdrawn,
  They slumber in secrecy.

Two worlds they have — a globe forgot
  Wheeling from dark to light;
And all the enchanted realm of dream
  That burgeons out of night.

MARTHA

"Once . . . once upon a time . . ."
  Over and over again,
Martha would tell us her stories,
  In the hazel glen.

Hers were those clear grey eyes
  You watch, and the story seems
Told by their beautifulness
  Tranquil as dreams.

She would sit with her two slim hands
  Clasped round her bended knees;
While we on our elbows lolled,
  And stared at ease.

Her voice, her narrow chin,
  Her grave small lovely head,
Seemed half the meaning
  Of the words she said.

"Once . . . once upon a time . . ."
    Like a dream you dream in the night,
Fairies and gnomes stole out
    In the leaf-green light.

And her beauty far away
    Would fade, as her voice ran on,
Till hazel and summer sun
    And all were gone:

All fordone and forgot;
    And like clouds in the height of the sky,
Our hearts stood still in the hush
    Of an age gone by.

SUPPOSE

"Suppose . . . and . . . suppose that a wild
little Horse of Magic
Came cantering out of the sky,
With bridle of silver, and into the saddle I
mounted,
To fly — and to fly;

"And we stretched up into the air, fleeting on in
the sunshine —
A speck in the gleam —
On galloping hoofs, his mane in the wind out-
flowing,
In a shadowy stream;

"And, oh, when, all lone, the gentle star of
evening
Came crinkling into the blue,
A magical castle we saw in the air, like a cloud of
moonlight,
As onward we flew;

· 33 ·

"And across the green moat on the drawbridge
    we foamed and we snorted,
        And *there* was a beautiful Queen
Who smiled at me strangely; and spoke to my
    wild little Horse, too —
        A lovely and beautiful Queen;

"And she cried with delight — and delight —
    to her delicate maidens,
        ' Behold my daughter — my dear!'
And they crowned me with flowers, and then to
    their harps sate playing,
        Solemn and clear;

"And magical cakes and goblets were spread on
    the table;
        And at window the birds came in,
Hopping along with bright eyes, pecking crumbs
    from the platters,
        And sipped of the wine;

"And splashing up — up to the roof tossed
    fountain of crystal;
        And Princes in scarlet and green

Shot with their bows and arrows, and kneeled
with their dishes
Of fruits for the Queen;

"And we walked in a magical garden with rivers
and bowers,
And my bed was of ivory and gold;
And the Queen breathed soft in my ear a song of
enchantment —
And I never grew old;

"And I never, never came back to the earth, oh,
never and never. . . .
How mother would cry and cry!
There'd be snow on the fields then, and all these
sweet flowers in the winter,
Would wither, and die. . . .
"Suppose . . . and suppose . . ."

THE UNFINISHED DREAM

Rare and sweet the air in that unimagined
    country —
  My spirit had wandered far
From its weary body close-enwrapt in slumber
  Where its home and earth-friends are;

A milk-like air — and of light all abundance;
  And there a river clear
Painting the scene like a picture on its bosom,
  Green foliage drifting near.

No sign of life I saw, as I pressed onward,
  Fish, nor beast, nor bird,
Till I came to a hill clothed in flowers to its
    summit,
  Then shrill small voices I heard.

And I saw from concealment a company of elf-
    folk
  With faces strangely fair,
Talking their unearthly scattered talk together,
  A bind of green grasses in their hair,

Marvellously gentle, feater far than children,
  In gesture, mien and speech,
Hastening onward in translucent shafts of sun-
    shine,
  And gossiping each with each.

Straw-light their locks, on neck and shoulder
    falling,
  Faint of almond the silks they wore,
Spun not of worm, but as if inwoven of moon-
    beams
  And foam on rock-bound shore;

Like lank-legged grasshoppers in June-tide
    meadows,
  Amalillios of the day,
Hungrily gazed upon by me — a stranger,
  In unknown regions astray.

Yet, happy beyond words, I marked their sunlit
    faces,
  Stealing soft enchantment from their eyes,
Tears in my own confusing their small image,
  Hearkening their bird-like cries.

They passed me, unseeing, a waft of flocking
    linnets;
  Sadly I fared on my way;
And came in my dream to a dream-like habita-
    tion,
  Close-shut, festooned, and grey.

Pausing, I gazed at the porch dust-still, vine-
    wreathèd,
  Worn the stone steps thereto,
Mute hung its bell, whence a stony head looked
    downward,
  Grey 'gainst the sky's pale-blue —

Strange to me: strange . . .

THE MASSACRE

The shadow of a poplar tree
  Lay in that lake of sun,
As I with my little sword went in —
  Against a thousand, one.

Haughty and infinitely armed,
  Insolent in their wrath,
Plumed high with purple plumes they held
  The narrow meadow path.

The air was sultry; all was still;
  The sun like flashing glass;
And snip-snap my light-whispering steel
  In arcs of light did pass.

Lightly and dull fell each proud head,
  Spiked keen without avail,
Till swam my uncontented blade
  With ichor green and pale.

And silence fell: the rushing sun
    Stood still in paths of heat,
Gazing in waves of horror on
    The dead about my feet.

Never a whir of wing, no bee
    Stirred o'er the shameful slain;
Nought but a thirsty wasp crept in,
    Stooped, and came out again.

The very air trembled in fear;
    Eclipsing shadow seemed
Rising in crimson waves of gloom —
    On one who dreamed.

THE CHILDREN OF STARE

Winter is fallen early
On the house of Stare;
Birds in reverberating flocks
Haunt its ancestral box;
Bright are the plenteous berries
In clusters in the air.

Still is the fountain's music,
The dark pool icy still,
Whereon a small and sanguine sun
Floats in a mirror on,
Into a West of crimson,
From a South of daffodil.

'Tis strange to see young children
In such a wintry house;
Like rabbits' on the frozen snow
Their tell-tale footprints go;
Their laughter rings like timbrels
'Neath evening ominous:

Their small and heightened faces
Like wine-red winter buds;
Their frolic bodies gentle as
    Flakes in the air that pass,
    Frail as the twirling petal
    From the briar of the woods.

Above them silence lours,
    Still as an arctic sea;
Light fails; night falls; the wintry moon
    Glitters; the crocus soon
    Will ope grey and distracted
    On earth's austerity:

Thick mystery, wild peril,
    Law like an iron rod: —
Yet sport they on in Spring's attire,
    Each with his tiny fire
    Blown to a core of ardour
    By the awful breath of God.

REVERIE

Bring not bright candles, for his eyes
  In twilight have sweet company;
Bring not bright candles, else they fly —
  His phantoms fly —
Gazing aggrieved on thee!

Bring not bright candles, startle not
  The phantoms of a vacant room,
Flocking above a child that dreams —
  Deep, deep in dreams, —
Hid, in the gathering gloom!

Bring not bright candles to those eyes
  That between earth and stars descry,
Lovelier for the shadows there,
  Children of air,
Palaces in the sky!

MUSIC

When music sounds, gone is the earth I know,
And all her lovely things even lovelier grow;
Her flowers in vision flame, her forest trees,
Lift burdened branches, stilled with ecstacies.

When music sounds, out of the water rise
Naiads whose beauty dims my waking eyes,
Rapt in strange dreams burns each enchanted
    face,
With solemn echoing stirs their dwelling-place.

When music sounds, all that I was I am
Ere to this haunt of brooding dust I came;
While from Time's woods break into distant
    song
The swift-winged hours, as I hasten along.

THE MERMAIDS

Sand, sand — hills of sand;
And the wind where nothing is
Green and sweet of the land;
No grass, no trees,
No bird, no butterfly,
But hills, hills of sand,
And a burning sky.

Sea, sea — mounds of the sea;
Hollow, and dark, and blue,
Flashing incessantly
The whole sea through;
No flower, no jutting root,
Only the floor of the sea,
With foam afloat.

Blow, blow, windingshells;
And the watery fish,
Deaf to the hidden bells,
In the water plash;

· 45 ·

No streaming gold, no eyes,
    Watching along the waves,
But far-blown shells, faint bells,
    From the darkling caves.

THE LITTLE SALAMANDER
TO MARGOT

When I go free,
I think 'twill be
A night of stars and snow,
And the wild fires of frost shall light
My footsteps as I go;
Nobody — nobody will be there
With groping touch, or sight,
To see me in my bush of hair
Dance burning through the night.

WILD TIME

Now silent falls the clacking mill;
Sweet — sweeter smells the briar;
The dew wells big on bud and twig;
The glow-worm's wrapt in fire.

Then sing, lully, lullay, with me,
And softly, lill-lall-lo, love,
'Tis high time, and wild time,
And no time, no, love!

The Western sky has vailed her rose,
The night-wind to the willow
Sigheth, "Now lovely, lean thy head,
Thy tresses be my pillow!"

Then sing, lully, lullay, with me,
And softly, lill-lall-lo, love,
Tis high time, and wild time,
And no time, no, love!

· 48 ·

Cries in the brake, bells in the sea:
The moon o'er moor and mountain
Cruddles her light from height to height,
Bedazzles pool and fountain.
Leap, fox; hoot, owl; wail, warbler sweet;
'Tis midnight now's a-brewing;
The fairy mob is all abroad;
And witches at their wooing.

Then sing, lully, lullay, with me,
And softly, lull-lall-lo, love,
'Tis high time, and wild time,
And no time, no, love!

WINTER

Green Mistletoe!
Oh, I remember now
A dell of snow,
Frost on the bough;
None there but I:
Snow, snow, and a wintry sky.

None there but I,
And footprints one by one,
Zigzaggedly,
Where I had run;
Where, shrill and powdery,
A robin sat in the tree.

And he whistled sweet;
And I in the crusted snow
With snow-clubbed feet
Jigged to and fro,
Till, from the day,
The rose-light ebbed away.

And the robin flew
Into the air — the air,
The white mist through;
And small and rare
The night-frost fell
Into the calm and misty dell.

And the dusk gathered low,
And the silver moon and stars
On the frozen snow
Drew taper bars,
Kindled winking fires
In the hooded briers.

And the sprawling Bear
Growled deep in the sky;
And Orion's hair
Streamed sparkling by:
But the North sighed low,
"Snow, snow, more snow!"

THE SLEEPER

As Ann came in one summer's day,
　　She felt that she must creep,
So silent was the clear cool house,
　　It seemed a house of sleep.
And sure, when she pushed open the door,
　　Rapt in the stillness there,
Her mother sat, with stooping head,
　　Asleep upon a chair;
Fast-fast asleep; her two hands laid
　　Loose-folded on her knee,
So that her small unconscious face
　　Looked half unreal to be:
So calmly lit with sleep's pale light
　　Each feature was; so fair
Her forehead — every trouble was
　　Smoothed out beneath her hair.
But though her mind in dream now moved,
　　Still seemed her gaze to rest —

From out beneath her fast-sealed lids,
   Above her moving breast —
On Ann; as quite, quite still she stood;
   Yet slumber lay so deep
Even her hands upon her lap
   Seemed saturate with sleep.
And as Ann peeped, a cloudlike dread
   Stole over her, and then,
On stealthy, mouselike feet she trod
   And tiptoed out again.

OLD SUSAN

When Susan's work was done, she would sit,
With one fat guttering candle lit,
And window opened wide to win
The sweet night air to enter in.
There, with a thumb to keep her place,
She would read, with stern and wrinkled face,
Her mild eyes gliding very slow
Across the letters to and fro,
While wagged the guttering candle flame
In the wind that through the window came.
And sometimes in the silence she
Would mumble a sentence audibly,
Or shake her head as if to say,
"You silly souls, to act this way!"
And never a sound from night I would hear,
Unless some far-off cock crowed clear;
Or her old shuffling thumb should turn
Another page; and, rapt and stern,

Through her great glasses bent on me,
She would glance into reality;
And shake her round old silvery head,
With — "You! — I thought you was in bed!"
Only to tilt her book again,
And rooted in Romance remain.

MISS LOO

When thin-strewn memory I look through,
I see most clearly poor Miss Loo —
Her tabby cat, her cage of birds,
Her nose, her hair, her muffled words,
And how she would open her green eyes,
As if in some immense surprise,
Whenever as we sat at tea
She made some small remark to me.

'Tis always drowsy summer when
From out the past she comes again;
The westering sunshine in a pool
Floats in her parlour still and cool;
While the slim bird its lean wires shakes,
As into piercing song it breaks;
Till Peter's pale-green eyes ajar
Dream, wake; wake, dream, in one brief bar.
And I am sitting, dull and shy,
And she with gaze of vacancy,

And large hands folded on the tray,
Musing the afternoon away;
Her satin bosom heaving slow
With sighs that softly ebb and flow
And her plain face in such dismay,
It seems unkind to look her way:
Until all cheerful back will come
Her gentle gleaming spirit home:
And one would think that poor Miss Loo
Asked nothing else, if she had you.

THE VEIL

I think and think; yet still I fail —
Why does this lady wear a veil?
Why thus elect to mask her face
Beneath that dainty web of lace?
The tip of a small nose I see,
And two red lips, set curiously
Like twin-born cherries on one stem,
And yet she has netted even them.
Her eyes, it's plain, survey with ease
Whate'er to glance upon they please.
Yet, whether hazel, grey, or blue,
Or that even lovelier lilac hue,
I cannot guess: why — why deny
Such beauty to the passer-by?
Out of a bush a nightingale
May expound his song; beneath that veil
A happy mouth no doubt can make
English sound sweeter for its sake.

But then, why muffle in, like this,
What every blossomy wind would kiss?
Why in that little night disguise
A daybreak face, those starry eyes?

THE BLIND BOY

"I have no master," said the Blind Boy,
  "My mother, 'Dame Venus' they do call;
Cowled in this hood she sent me begging
  For whate'er in pity may befall.

"Hard was her visage, me adjuring, —
  'Have no fond mercy on the kind!
Here be sharp arrows, bunched in quiver,
  Draw close ere striking — thou art blind.'

"So stand I here, my woes entreating,
  In this dark alley, lest the Moon
Point with her sparkling my barbed armoury
  Shine on my silver-lacèd shoon.

"Oh, sir, unkind this Dame to me-ward;
  Of the salt billow was her birth. . . .
In your sweet charity draw nearer
  The saddest rogue on Earth!"

FORGIVENESS

"O thy flamed cheek,
  Those locks with weeping wet,
Eyes that, forlorn and meek,
  On mine are set.

"Poor hands, poor feeble wings,
  Folded, a-droop, O sad!
See, 'tis my heart that sings
  To make thee glad.

"My mouth breathes love, thou dear.
  All that I am and know
Is thine.   My breast — draw near:
  Be grieved not so!"

MRS. GRUNDY

"Step very softly, sweet Quiet-foot,
Stumble not, whisper not, smile not:
By this dark ivy stoop cheek and brow.
Still even thy heart! What seest thou? . . ."

"High-coifed, broad-browed, aged, suave yet
    grim,
A large flat face, eyes keenly dim,
Staring at nothing — that's me! — and yet,
With a hate one could never, oh, never for-
    get. . . ."

"This is my world, my garden, my home,
Hither my father bade mother to come
And bear me out of the dark into light,
And happy I was in her tender sight.

"And then, thou frail flower, she died and went,
Forgetting my pitiless banishment,
And that Old Woman — an Aunt — she said,
Came hither, lodged, fattened, and made her
    bed.

"Oh, yes, thou most blessed, from Monday to
  Sunday,
Has lived on me, preyed on me, Mrs. Grundy:
Called me, 'dear Nephew'; on each of those
  chairs
Has gloated in righteousness, heard my prayers.

"Why didst thou dare the thorns of the grove,
Timidest trespasser, huntress of love?
Now thou hast peeped, and now dost know
What kind of creature is thine for foe.

"Not that she'll tear out thy innocent eyes,
Poison thy mouth with deviltries.
Watch thou, wait thou: soon will begin
The guile of a voice: hark! . . ." "Come in,
  Come in!"

AUTUMN

There is wind where the rose was;
Cold rain where sweet grass was;
  And clouds like sheep
  Stream o'er the steep
Grey skies where the lark was.

Nought gold where your hair was;
Nought warm where your hand was;
  But phantom, forlorn,
  Beneath the thorn,
Your ghost where your face was.

Sad winds where your voice was;
Tears, tears where my heart was;
  And ever with me,
  Child, ever with me,
Silence where hope was.

WINTER DUSK

Dark frost was in the air without,
  The dusk was still with cold and gloom,
When less than even a shadow came
  And stood within the room.

But of the three around the fire,
  None turned a questioning head to look,
Still read a clear voice, on and on,
  Still stooped they o'er their book.

The children watched their mother's eyes
  Moving on softly line to line;
It seemed to listen too — that shade,
  Yet made no outward sign.

The fire-flames crooned a tiny song,
  No cold wind moved the wintry tree;
The children both in Faërie dreamed
  Beside their mother's knee.

And nearer yet that spirit drew
Above that heedless one, intent
Only on what the simple words
Of her small story meant.

No voiceless sorrow grieved her mind,
No memory her bosom stirred,
Nor dreamed she, as she read to two,
'Twas surely three who heard.

Yet when — the story done — she smiled
From face to face, serene and clear,
A love, half dread, sprang up, as she
Leaned close and drew them near.

THE GHOST

"Who knocks?"   "I, who was beautiful,
  Beyond all dreams to restore,
I, from the roots of the dark thorn am hither,
  And knock on the door."

"Who speaks?"   "I — once was my speech
  Sweet as the bird's on the air.
When echo lurks by the waters to heed;
  'Tis I speak thee fair."

"Dark is the hour!"   "Ay, and cold."
  "Lone is my house."   "Ah, but mine?"
"Sight, touch, lips, eyes yearned in vain."
  "Long dead these to thine. . . ."

Silence.   Still faint on the porch
  Brake the flames of the stars.
In gloom groped a hope-wearied hand
  Over keys, bolts, and bars.

A face peered.   All the grey night
In chaos of vacancy shone;
Nought but vast sorrow was there —
The sweet cheat gone.

THE QUIET ENEMY

Hearken — now the hermit bee
Drones a quiet threnody;
Greening on the stagnant pool
The criss-cross light slants silken-cool;
In the venomed yew tree wings
Preen and flit.   The linnet sings.

Gradually the brave sun
Drops to a day's journey done;
In the marshy flats abide
Mists to muffle midnight-tide.
Puffed within the belfry tower
Hungry owls drowse out their hour . . .

Walk in beauty.   Vaunt thy rose.
Flaunt thy transient loveliness.
Pace for pace with thee there goes
A shape that hath not come to bless.
I thine enemy? . . . Nay, nay.
I can only watch and wait
Patient treacherous time away,
Hold ajar the wicket gate.

THE OWL

What if to edge of dream,
When the spirit is come,
Shriek the hunting owl,
And summon it home —
To the fear-stirred heart
And the ancient dread
Of man, when cold root or stone
Pillowed roofless head?

Clangs not at last the hour
When roof shelters not;
And the ears are deaf,
And all fears forgot:
Since the spirit too far has fared
For summoning scream
Of any strange fowl on earth
To shatter its dream?

FUTILITY

Sink, thou strange heart, unto thy rest.
Pine now no more, to pine in vain.
Doth not the moon on heaven's breast
Call the floods home again?

Doth not the summer faint at last?
Do not her restless rivers flow,
When that her transient day is past,
To hide them in ice and snow?

All this — thy world — an end shall make?
Planet to sun return again;
The universe, to sleep from wake,
In a last peace remain?

Alas, the futility of care
That, spinning thought to thought, doth weave
An idle argument on the air
We love not, nor believe.

THE FAMILIAR

"Are you far away?"
"Yea, I am far — far;
Where the green wave shelves to the sand,
And the rainbows are;
And an ageless sun beats fierce
From an empty sky:
There, O thou Shadow forlorn,
Is the wraith of thee, I."

"Are you happy, most Lone?"
"Happy, forsooth!
Who am eyes of the air; voice of the foam;
Ah, happy in truth.
My hair is astream, this cheek
Glistens like silver, and see,
As the gold to the dross, the ghost in the mirk,
I am calling to thee."

"Nay, I am bound,
And your cry faints out in my mind,
Peace not on earth have I found,
Yet to earth am resigned.
Cease thy shrill mockery, Voice,
Nor answer again."
"O Master, thick cloud shuts thee out
And cold tempests of rain."

THE OLD MEN

Old and alone, sit we,
   Caged, riddle-rid men;
Lost to Earth's "Listen!" and "See!"
   Thought's "Wherefore?" and "When?"

Only far memories stray
   Of a past once lovely, but now
Wasted and faded away,
   Like green leaves from the bough.

Vast broods the silence of night,
   The ruinous moon
Lifts on our faces her light,
   Whence all dreaming is gone.

We speak not; trembles each head;
   In their sockets our eyes are still;
Desire as cold as the dead;
   Without wonder or will.

And One, with a lanthorn, draws near,
    At clash with the moon in our eyes:
"Where art thou?" he asks. "I am here."
    One by one we arise.

And none lifts a hand to withhold
    A friend from the touch of that foe:
Heart cries unto heart, "Thou art old!"
    Yet, reluctant, we go.

IN THE DOCK

Pallid, mis-shapen he stands. The world's
    grimed thumb,
Now hooked securely in his matted hair,
Has haled him struggling from his poisonous
    slum
And flung him mute as fish close-netted there.
His bloodless hands entalon that iron rail.
He gloats in beastlike trance.   His settling eyes,
From staring face to face rove on — and quail.
Justice for carrion pants, and these the flies.

Voice after voice in smooth impartial drone
Erects horrific in his darkening brain
A timber framework, where agape, alone
Bright life will kiss good-bye the cheek of Cain.
Sudden like wolf he cries; and sweats to see
When howls man's soul, it howls inaudibly.

DRUGGED

Inert in his chair,
In a candle's guttering glow;
His bottle empty,
His fire sunk low;
With drug-sealed lids shut fast,
Unsated mouth ajar,
This darkened phantasm walks
Where nightmares are:

In a frenzy of life and light,
Crisscross — a menacing throng —
They gibe, they squeal at the stranger,
Jostling along,
Their faces cadaverous grey.
While on high from an attic stare
Horrors, in beauty apparelled,
Down the dark air.

· 77 ·

A stream gurgles over its stones,
The chambers within are a-fire.
Stumble his shadowy feet
Through shine, through mire;
And the flames leap higher.
In vain yelps the wainscot mouse;
In vain beats the hour;
Vacant, his body must drowse
Until daybreak shall flower —

Staining these walls with its rose,
And the draughts of the morning shall stir
Cold on cold brow, cold hands;
And the wanderer
Back to flesh house must return —
Lone soul — in horror to see,
Than dream more meagre and awful,
Reality.

ANATOMY

By chance my fingers, resting on my face,
  Stayed suddenly where in its orbit shone
  The lamp of all things beautiful; then on,
Following more heedfully, did softly trace
Each arch and prominence and hollow place
  That shall revealed be when all else is gone —
  Warmth, colour, roundness — to oblivion,
And nothing left but darkness and disgrace.

Life like a moment passed seemed then to be;
  A transient dream this raiment that it wore;
While spelled my hand out its mortality
  Made certain all that had seemed doubt be-
  fore:
Proved — O how vaguely, yet how lucidly! —
  How much death does; and yet can do no
  more.

· 79 ·

THE SUICIDE

Did these night-hung houses,
Of quiet, starlit stone,
Breathe not a whisper of — 'Stay,
Thou unhappy one;
Whither so secret away?'

Sighed not the unfriending wind,
Chill with nocturnal dew,
'Pause, pause, in thy haste,
O thou distraught! I too
Tryst with the Atlantic waste.'

Steep fell the drowsy street;
In slumber the world was blind:
Breathed not one midnight flower
Peace in thy broken mind? —
'Brief, yet sweet, is life's hour.'

Syllabled thy last tide —
By as dark moon stirred,
And doomed to forlorn unrest —
Not one compassionate word? . . .
        'Cold is this breast.'

NOT THAT WAY

No, no. Guard thee.   Get thee gone.
            Not that way.
See; the louring clouds glide on,
Skirting West to South; and see,
The green light under that sycamore tree —
            Not that way.

There the leaden trumpets blow,
            Solemn and slow.
There the everlasting walls
Frown above the waterfalls
            Silver and cold;
            Timelessly old:
            Not that way.

Not toward Death, who, stranger, fairer,
Than any siren turns his head —
Than sea-couched siren, arched with rainbows,
Where knell the waves of her ocean bed.

Alas, that beauty hangs her flowers
For lure of his demoniac powers:
Alas, that from these eyes should dart
Such piercing summons to thy heart;
That mine in frenzy of longing beats,
Still lusting for these gross deceits.
                    Not that way!

EVEN IN THE GRAVE

I laid my inventory at the hand
  Of Death, who in his gloomy arbour sate;
  And while he conned it, sweet and desolate
I heard Love singing in that quiet land.
He read the record even to the end —
  The heedless, livelong injuries of Fate,
  The burden of foe, the burden of love and
    hate;
The wounds of foe, the bitter wounds of friend:

All, all, he read, ay, even the indifference,
  The vain talk, vainer silence, hope and dream.
He questioned me: "What seek'st thou then
    instead?"
  I bowed my face in the pale evening gleam.
Then gazed he on me with strange innocence:
  "Even in the grave thou wilt have thyself,"
    he said.

WHO?

1st Stranger.	Who walks with us on the hills ?
2nd Stranger.	I cannot see for the mist.
3rd Stranger.	Running water I hear,
	Keeping lugubrious tryst
	With its cresses and grasses and weeds,
	In the white obscure light from the sky.
2nd Stranger.	*Who walks with us on the hills?*
Wild Birds.	Ay! . . . Aye! . . . Ay! . . .

THE MOTH

Isled in the midnight air,
Musked with the dark's faint bloom,
Out into glooming and secret haunts
    The flame cries, "Come!"

Lovely in dye and fan,
A-tremble in shimmering grace,
A moth from her winter swoon
    Uplifts her face:

Stares from her glamorous eyes;
Wafts her on plumes like mist;
In ecstasy swirls and sways
    To her strange tryst.

THE UNCHANGING

After the songless rose of evening,
   Night quiet, dark, still,
In nodding cavalcade advancing
   Starred the deep hill:
You, in the valley standing,
   In your quiet wonder took
All that glamour, peace, and mystery
   In one grave look.
Beauty hid your naked body,
   Time dreamed in your bright hair,
In your eyes the constellations
   Burned far and fair.

GOLD

Sighed the wind to the wheat:
"The Queen who is slumbering there,
Once bewildered the rose;
Scorned, 'Thou un-fair!'
Once, from that bird-whirring court,
Ascended the ruinous stair.
Aloft, on that weed-hung turret, suns
Smote on her hair —
Of a gold by Archiac sought,
Of a gold sea-hid,
Of a gold that from core of quartz
No flame shall bid
Pour into light of the air
For God's Jews to see."

Mocked the wheat to the wind:
"Kiss me! Kiss me!"

FLOTSAM

Screamed the far sea-mew. On the mirroring
    sands
Bell-shrill the oyster-catchers. Burned the sky.
Couching my cheeks upon my sun-scorched
    hands,
Down from bare rock I gazed. The sea swung
    by.

Dazzling dark blue and verdurous, quiet with
    snow,
Empty with loveliness, with music a-roar,
Her billowing summits heaving noon-aglow —
Crashed the Atlantic on the cliff-ringed shore.

Drowsed by the tumult of that moving deep,
Sense into outer silence fainted, fled ;
And rising softly, from the fields of sleep,
Stole to my eyes a lover from the dead ;

Crying an incantation — learned, Where? When?

White swirled the foam, a fount, a blinding gleam

Of ice-cold breast, cruel eyes, wild mouth — and then

A still dirge echoing on from dream to dream.

THE DECOY

'Tell us, O pilgrim, what strange She
Lures and decoys your wanderings on?
Cheek, eye, brow, lip, you scan each face,
Smile, ponder — and are gone.

'Are we not flesh and blood?   Mark well,
We touch you with our hands.   We speak
A tongue that may earth's secrets tell:
Why further will you seek?'

'Far have I come, and far must fare.
Noon and night and morning-prime,
I search the long road, bleak and bare,
That fades away in Time.

'On the world's brink its wild weeds shake,
And there my own dust, dark with dew,
Burns with a rose that, sleep or wake,
Beckons me "Follow true!"'

'Her name, crazed soul?   And her degree?
What peace, prize, profit in her breast?'
'A thousand cheating names hath she;
And none fore-tokens rest.'

THE OLD ANGLER

Twilight leaned mirrored in a pool
   Where willow boughs swept green and hoar,
Silk-clear the water, calm and cool,
   Silent the weedy shore:

There in abstracted, brooding mood
   One fishing sate. His painted float
Motionless as a planet stood;
   Motionless his boat.

A melancholy soul was this,
   With lantern jaw, gnarled hand, vague eye;
Huddled in pensive solitariness
   He had fished existence by.

Empty his creel; stolen his bait —
   Impassively he angled on,
Though mist now showed the evening late
   And daylight well-nigh gone.

Suddenly, like a tongueless bell,
  Downward his gaudy cork did glide;
A deep, low-gathering, gentle swell
  Spread slowly far and wide.

Wheeped out his tackle from noiseless winch,
  And furtive as a thief, his thumb,
With nerve intense, wound inch by inch
  A line no longer numb.

What fabulous spoil could thus unplayed
  Gape upward to a mortal air? —
He stoops engrossed; his tanned cheek greyed;
  His heart stood still: for there,

Wondrously fairing, beneath the skin
  Of secretly bubbling water seen,
Swims — not the silver of scale and fin —
  But gold immixt with green.

Deeply astir in oozy bed,
  The darkening mirror ripples and rocks:
And lo — a wan-pale, lovely head,
  Hook tangled in its locks!

Cold from her haunt — a naiad slim.
  Shoulder and cheek gleamed ivory white;
Though now faint stars stood over him,
  The hour hard on night.

Her green eyes gazed like one half-blind
  In sudden radiance; her breast
Breathed the sweet air, while gently twined,
  'Gainst the cold water pressed,

Her lean webbed hands. She floated there,
  Light as a scentless petalled flower,
Water-drops dewing from her hair
  In tinkling beadlike shower.

So circling sidelong, her tender throat
  Uttered a grieving, desolate wail;
Shrill o'er the dark pool lapsed its note,
  Piteous as nightingale.

Ceased Echo. And he? — a life's remorse
  Welled to a tongue unapt to charm,
But never a word broke harsh and hoarse
  To quiet her alarm.

With infinite stealth his twitching thumb
   Tugged softly at the tautened gut,
Bubble-light, fair, her lips now dumb,
   She moved, and struggled not;

But with set, wild, unearthly eyes
   Pale-gleaming, fixed as if in fear,
She couched in the water, with quickening sighs,
   And floated near.

In hollow heaven the stars were at play;
   Wan glow-worms greened the pool-side grass;
Dipped the wide-bellied boat.   His prey
   Gazed on; nor breathed.   Alas! —

Long sterile years had come and gone;
   Youth, like a distant dream, was sped;
Heart, hope, and eyes had hungered on . . .
   He turned a shaking head,

And clumsily groped amid the gold,
   Sleek with night dews, of that tangling hair,
Till pricked his finger keen and cold
   The barb imbedded there.

Teeth clenched, he drew his knife — '*Snip,
   snip*,' —
  Groaned, and sate shivering back; and she,
Treading the water with birdlike dip,
  Shook her sweet shoulders free;

Drew backward, smiling, infatuate fair,
  His life's disasters in her eyes,
All longing and folly, grief, despair,
  Daydreams and mysteries.

She stooped her brow; laid low her cheek,
  And, steering on that silk-tressed craft,
Out from the listening, leaf-hung creek,
  Tossed up her chin, and laughed —

A mocking, icy, inhuman note.
  One instant flashed that crystal breast,
Leaned, and was gone. Dead-still the boat:
  And the deep dark at rest.

Flits moth to flower. A water-rat
  Noses the placid ripple. And lo!
Streams a lost meteor. Night is late,
  And daybreak zephyrs flow . . .

And he — the cheated ?   Dusk till morn,
  Insensate, even of hope forsook,
He muttering squats, aloof, forlorn,
  Dangling a baitless hook.

THE MOUNTAINS

Still, and blanched, and cold, and lone,
　The icy hills far off from me
With frostly ulys overgrown
　Stand in their sculptured secrecy.

No path of theirs the chamois fleet
　Treads, with a nostril to the wind;
O'er their ice-marbled glaciers beat
　No wings of eagles in my mind —

Yea, in my mind these mountains rise,
　Their perils dyed with evening's rose;
And still my ghost sits at my eyes
　And thirsts for their untroubled snows.

THULE

If thou art sweet as they are sad
  Who on the shores of Time's salt sea
Watch on the dim horizon fade
  Ships bearing love to night and thee;

If past all beacons Hope hath lit
  In the dark wanderings of the deep
They who unwilling traverse it
  Dream not till dawn unseal their sleep;

Ah, cease not in thy winds to mock
  Us, who yet wake, but cannot see
Thy distant shores; who at each shock
  Of the waves' onset faint for thee!

THE MONOLOGUE

Alas, O Lovely One,
    Imprisoned here,
I tap; thou answerest not,
    I doubt, and fear.
Yet transparent as glass these walls,
    If thou lean near.

Last dusk, at those high bars
    There came, scarce-heard,
Claws, fluttering feathers,
    Of deluded bird —
With one shrill, scared, faint note
    The silence stirred.

Rests in that corner,
    In puff of dust, a straw —
Vision of harvest-fields
    I never saw,
Of strange green streams and hills,
    Forbidden by law.

These things I whisper,
    For I see — in mind —

Thy caged cheek whiten
At the wail of wind,
That thin breast wasting; unto
Woe resigned.

Take comfort, listen!
Once we twain were free;
There was a Country —
Lost the memory . . .
Lay thy cold brow on hand,
And dream with me.

Awaits me torture,
I have smelt their rack;
From spectral groaning wheel
Have turned me back;
Thumbscrew and boot, and then —
The yawning sack.

Lean closer, then;
Lay palm on stony wall.
Let but thy ghost beneath
Thine eyelids call:

'Courage, my brother!'   Nought
    Can then appal.

    Yet coward, coward am **I**,
      And drink I must
    When clanks the pannikin
      With the longed-for crust;
Though heart within is sour
      With disgust.

    Long hours there are,
      When mutely tapping — well,
    Is it to Vacancy
      I these tidings tell?
Knock these numb fingers against
      An empty cell? . . .

    Nay, answer not.
      Let still mere longing make
    Thy presence sure to me,
      While in doubt I shake:
Be but my Faith in thee,
      For that faith's sake.

THE VOICE

'We are not often alone, we two,'
Mused a secret voice in my ear,
As the dying hues of afternoon
Lapsed into evening drear.

A withered leaf, wafted on in the street,
Like a wayless spectre, sighed;
Aslant on the roof-tops a sickly moon
Did mutely abide.

Yet waste though the shallowing day might
    seem,
And fainter than hope its rose,
Strangely that speech in my thoughts welled on;
As water in-flows:

Like remembered words once heard in a room
Wherein death kept far-away tryst;
'Not often alone, we two; but thou,
How sorely missed!'

ALL THAT'S PAST

Very old are the woods;
  And the buds that break
Out of the briar's boughs,
  When March winds wake,
So old with their beauty are —
  Oh, no man knows
Through what wild centuries
  Roves back the rose.

Very old are the brooks;
  And the rills that rise
Where snow sleeps cold beneath
  The azure skies
Sing such a history
  Of come and gone,
Their every drop is as wise
  As Solomon.

· 104 ·

Very old are we men;
  Our dreams are tales
Told in dim Eden
  By Eve's nightingales;
We wake and whisper awhile,
  But, the day gone by,
Silence and sleep like fields
  Of amaranth lie.

ARABIA

Far are the shades of Arabia,
  Where the Princes ride at noon,
'Mid the verdurous vales and thickets,
  Under the ghost of the moon;
And so dark is that vaulted purple
  Flowers in the forest rise
And toss into blossom 'gainst the phantom stars
  Pale in the noonday skies.

Sweet is the music of Arabia
  In my heart, when out of dreams
I still in the thin clear mirk of dawn
  Descry her gliding streams;
Hear her strange lutes on the green banks
  Ring loud with the grief and delight
Of the dim-silked dark-haired Musicians
  In the brooding silence of night.

They haunt me — her lutes and her forests;
  No beauty on earth I see
But shadowed with that dream recalls
  Her loveliness to me:

Still eyes look coldly upon me,
　　Cold voices whisper and say —
"He is crazed with the spell of far Arabia,
　　They have stolen his wits away."

THE LISTENERS

"Is there anybody there," said the Traveller,
    Knocking on the moonlit door;
And his horse in the silence champed the grasses
    Of the forest's ferny floor;
And a bird flew up out of the turret,
    Above the Traveller's head;
And he smote upon the door again a second time:
    "Is there anybody there?" he said.
But no one descended to the Traveller;
    No head from the leaf-fringed sill
Leaned over and looked into his grey eyes,
    Where he stood perplexed and still.
But only a host of phantom listeners
    That dwelt in the lone house then
Stood listening in the quiet of the moonlight
    To that voice from the world of men;
Stood thronging the faint moonbeams on the
    dark stair,

That goes down to the empty hall,
Hearkening in an air stirred and shaken
  By the lonely Traveller's call.
And he felt in his heart their strangeness,
  Their stillness answering his cry,
While his horse moved, cropping the dark turf,
  'Neath the starred and leafy sky;
For he suddenly smote on the door, even
  Louder, and lifted his head:
"Tell them I came, and no one answered,
  That I kept my word," he said.
Never the least stir made the listeners,
  Though every word he spake
Fell echoing through the shadowiness of the
    still house
  From the one man left awake:
Ay, they heard his foot upon the stirrup,
  And the sound of iron on stone,
And how the silence surged softly backward,
  When the plunging hoofs were gone.

ALEXANDER

It was the Great Alexander,
  Capped with a golden helm,
Sate in the ages, in his floating ship,
  In a dead calm.

Voices of sea-maids singing
  Wandered across the deep:
The sailors labouring on their oars
  Rowed, as in sleep.

All the high pomp of Asia,
  Charmed by that siren lay,
Out of their weary and dreaming minds,
  Faded away.

Like a bold boy sate their Captain,
  His glamour withered and gone,
In the souls of his brooding mariners,
  While the song pined on.

Time, like a falling dew,
  Life, like the scene of a dream,
Laid between slumber and slumber,
  Only did seem. . . .

O Alexander, then,
  In all us mortals too,
Wax thou not bold — too bold
  On the wave dark-blue!

Come the calm, infinite night,
  Who then will hear
Aught save the singing
  Of the sea-maids clear?

AN EPITAPH

Here lies a most beautiful lady,
Light of step and heart was she;
I think she was the most beautiful lady
That ever was in the West Country.
But beauty vanishes; beauty passes;
However rare — rare it be;
And when I crumble, who will remember
This lady of the West Country?

THE SCRIBE

What lovely things
  Thy hand hath made:
The smooth-plumed bird
  In its emerald shade,
The seed of the grass,
  The speck of stone
Which the wayfaring ant
  Stirs — and hastes on!
Though I should sit
  By some tarn in thy hills,
Using its ink
  As the spirit wills
To write of Earth's wonders,
  Its live, willed things,
Flit would the ages
  On soundless wings
Ere unto Z
  My pen drew nigh;

Leviathan told,
And the honey-fly:
And still would remain
My wit to try —
My worn reeds broken,
The dark tarn dry,
All words forgotten —
Thou, Lord, and I.

THE LAST COACHLOAD
(TO COLIN)

Crashed through the woods that lumbering
    Coach. The dust
Of flinted roads bepowdering felloe and hood.
Its gay paint cracked, its axles red with rust,
It lunged, lurched, toppled through a solitude

Of whispering boughs, and feathery 'nid-nod
    grass.
Plodded the fetlocked horses. Glum and mum,
Its ancient Coachman recked not where he was,
Nor into what strange haunt his wheels were
    come.

Crumbling the leather of his dangling reins;
Worn to a cow's tuft his stumped, idle whip;
Sharp eyes of beast and bird in the trees' green
    lanes
Gleamed out like stars above a derelict ship.

"Old Father Time — Time — Time!" jeered
    twittering throat.
A squirrel capered on the leader's rump,
Slithered a weasel, peered a thief-like stoat,
In sandy warren beat on the coney's thump.

Mute as a mammet in his saddle sate
The hunched Postilion, clad in magpie trim;
Buzzed the bright flies around his hairless pate;
Yaffle and jay squawked mockery at him.

Yet marvellous peace and amity breathed there.
Tranquil the labyrinths of this sundown wood.
Musking its chaces, bloomed the brier-rose fair;
Spellbound as if in trance the pine-trees stood.

Through moss and pebbled rut the wheels
    rasped on;
That Ancient drowsing on his box.   And still
The bracken track with glazing sunbeams shone;
Laboured the horses, straining at the hill. . . .

But now — a verdurous height with eve-shade
    sweet;
Far, far to West the Delectable Mountains glowed.

Above, Night's canopy; at the horses' feet
A sea-like honied waste of flowers flowed.
There fell a pause of utter quiet. And —
Out from one murky window glanced an eye,
Stole from the other a lean, groping hand,
The padded doors swung open with a sigh.

And — *Exeunt Omnes!* None to ask the fare —
A myriad human odds in a last release
Leap out incontinent, snuff the incensed air;
A myriad parched-up voices whisper, "Peace."

On, on, and on — a stream, a flood, they flow.
O wondrous vale of jocund buds and bells!
Like vanishing smoke the rainbow legions glow,
Yet still the enravished concourse sweeps and
    swells.

All journeying done. Rest now from lash and
    spur —
Laughing and weeping, shoulder and elbow —
    'twould seem
That Coach capacious all Infinity were,
And these the fabulous figments of a dream.

Mad for escape; frenzied each breathless mote,
Lest rouse the Old Enemy from his death-still
    swoon,
Lest crack that whip again — they fly, they
    float,
Scamper, breathe — "Paradise!" abscond, are
    gone. . . .

FAREWELL

When I lie where shades of darkness
  Shall no more assail mine eyes,
Nor the rain make lamentation
  When the wind sighs;
How will fare the world whose wonder
Was the very proof of me?
Memory fades, must the remembered
  Perishing be?

Oh, when this my dust surrenders
Hand, foot, lip, to dust again,
May these loved and loving faces
  Please other men!
May the rusting harvest hedgerow
Still the Traveller's Joy entwine,
And as happy children gather
  Posies once mine.

Look thy last on all things lovely,
Every hour.   Let no night
Seal thy sense in deathly slumber
  Till to delight
Thou have paid thy utmost blessing;
Since that all things thou wouldst praise
Beauty took from those who loved them
  In other days.